Festivals

HALLOWE'EN

Robin May

Festivals

Buddhist Festivals
Christmas
Easter
Hallowe'en
Harvest and Thanksgiving
Hindu Festivals
Jewish Festivals
Muslim Festivals
New Year
Sikh Festivals

First published in 1984 by
Wayland (Publishers) Limited
61 Western Road, Hove
East Sussex BN3 1JD, England

Second impression 1985
Third impression 1986

ISBN 0 85078 467 0

Phototypeset by The Grange Press, Southwick, Sussex
Printed and bound in Italy by G. Canale & C. S.p.A., Turin

Contents

Hallowe'en celebrations

A very old festival

Hallowe'en! A time for games, fun and fortune-telling, for ghost stories and making mischief. At Hallowe'en on 31 October, millions of people celebrate a very old festival indeed.

For centuries, people believed that Hallowe'en was a night when witches walked – or flew! – and ghosts and spirits were on the loose. Ordinary folk also believed that they could see into the future.

For hundreds of years, the thought of witches has frightened people at Hallowe'en.

Hallowe'en has always been a good excuse to play games and have fun.

Today, many people say that Hallowe'en is just an excuse for a good time. After all, who believes in ghosts and magic nowadays?

In fact, many people do. Yet what makes Hallowe'en so special is its long and colourful history. For all the fun and games, it is part of the story of Britain, Ireland and northern France – part of our 2,000-year-old Celtic past. It belongs to North America, too.

Hallowe'en was originally known as the Festival of the Dead, and it had a strong hold on our Celtic and Saxon ancestors. The Church wanted to break this hold, and to do this called it All Hallows' Eve, 'hallow' meaning holy, or holy man or saint. This later became Hallowe'en, and the Church made 1 November All Saints' Day. But Hallowe'en was and still is more a 'heathen' festival than a Christian one, as we shall see.

A frightening fifteenth-century picture of witches, devils and evil spirits.

A night of fun and frights

Hallowe'en is fun now, and sometimes can be quite frightening. It was the other way round in the past, and often the 'fun' was quite rough. For example, 150 years ago in Scotland, the youngsters would attack each other's bonfires with sticks and stones in order to wreck them! As we shall see, fire played a big part in the Hallowe'en story. So did fortune-telling.

In the past, a girl would stick apple pips on her cheek. Each pip stood for one of her sweethearts, and as the pips fell off the girl knew which sweethearts to get rid of until there was only one left! While waiting for the pips to fall off, the girl would say:

> Pippin, pippin, I stick thee there,
> That that is true, thou mayest declare!

Meanwhile, the chances were that a nearby cottage door would be unlatched and inside there would be food on the table. The family put it there for their dead relatives to enjoy who, they believed, would visit them. The fire would be alight so that the spirits could warm themselves. This was supposed to make the coming winter easier for spirits to bear.

Ordinary folk believed that terrors were abroad that night, one horrible Welsh phantom being the tailless 'black sow'. This fiend was expected to appear after a good time had been had by all around a hilltop bonfire. When the fire was dying, everyone ran down the hill shouting: 'May the tailless black sow take the hindmost!'

Meanwhile, in Hertfordshire and elsewhere, lanterns were kept burning all night in order to keep foul fiends out, just in case.

In Scotland, youngsters used to wreck each other's bonfires with sticks and stones.

Once upon a time

The Celts were mainly farmers, raising cattle and working the land.

The festival of Samhain

When the Romans first came to Britain in 55 BC, they found people called Celts there. The Celts had two seasons, winter from November to May, then summer. And to them, the first day of November was not only the first day of winter, it was also the first day of the new year. This the Celts celebrated with the festival of Samhain (or Samhuin), their New Year's Eve. (Samhain means 'summer's end' in Celtic.) The Celts also had a spring festival called Beltane, our May Day.

The Celts gave thanks for their harvest on Samhain, but it was also a festival of the dead. It was a time when vegetation was dying. Life and crops would return early in the summer.

There was feasting at Samhain, also human sacrifice. Food was left for the dead as everyone believed that they would return on that night! Everyone was frightened, and tried to avoid the visiting ghosts. Sometimes they ate the food that the ghosts were meant to share. This is commemorated at Knutsford in Cheshire, where 'soul' cakes are eaten by candle-light – light that is supposed to guide the spirits back to their old homes.

The Celts tried to make peace with each other at Samhain, just as we try to at Christmas. Later, in the AD 800s, the Church made All Saints' Day – 1 November – a Christian Samhain, and All Souls' Day, 2 November, a day to remember the dead. All Hallows' Eve was an attempt to Christianize Hallowe'en, but it failed.

The Celts sacrificed humans at the festival of Samhain.

Hallow Tide

Though Hallowe'en is not itself a true Christian festival, the Church, as we have seen, 'attached' itself to the pagan feast. As far back as the seventh century, there was a special feast for all the saints in heaven on 13 May. The Church switched this feast to 1 November in AD 834, calling it All Saints' Day.

So it came about that on 1 November the saints of the Church were suitably celebrated, and still are. The great English composer, Ralph Vaughan Wiliams, was to write one of the most stirring of

Sugar skulls like this one are eaten on All Souls' Day in Mexico.

Christians honour the dead at Hallow Tide.

all tunes for the hymn, 'For All the Saints', more than a thousand years later.

In AD 988, it was decided that 2 November would be known as All Souls' Day. On this day, the Church remembers all faithful Christians who have died. It is a day when many Roman Catholics offer prayer for those still in purgatory who have not yet been blessed by reaching heaven and God.

In this way, Hallowe'en – All Hallows' Eve – became the start of Hallow Tide, 'Tide' meaning time. Christianity honoured the dead – certainly more reverentially than the lively festival of Hallowe'en.

The popularity of All Saints' Day is such that many hundreds of British churches have been named All Saints. And one of the most famous of Oxford colleges bears the name All Souls.

The 'little people'

A seventeenth-century picture of the 'little people' dancing in a circle.

Once, the Celts believed that the people who had inhabited Britain before them were the 'little people'. The little people were supposed to know all about herbs and poisons in a way that their enemies did not, and could 'vanish' into the landscape without a trace. It is not surprising, then, that the Celts came to believe that the little people had magical powers. They also thought that Samhain and Midsummer Eve were big nights for the little people.

The Romans, who conquered the Celts, also came to believe that the countryside was full of the

Pomona (centre) was the Roman goddess of trees and fruit.

little people. They thought that not all these mysterious folk were hostile, but that they had the power to frighten them.

Being practical people, the Romans also combined two of their festivals with the Celtic Samhain. 'Feralia' honoured the dead in late October, while 'Pomona' honoured the goddess of trees and fruit. That may well be the reason why apples, more than any other fruit, are connected with Hallowe'en.

People believed in the existence of the little people long after the Romans left Britain, and even today there are people who believe that the little people exist. Many of those enchanted folk from fairy tales stem from these little people, including such favourites as fairies and goblins.

Fairy places

If one of our ancestors offered another one a trip to fairyland, he or she would think the other mad! No night was more dangerous than Hallowe'en, for it was believed one could be snatched away for ever by fairies.

A seventeenth-century register of death has three people frightened to death by fairies, and one led into a horsepond by a will-o'-the-wisp.

As for being snatched from the real world to fairyland – a hazard in ancient Scotland, so they say – there was a chance of getting back. The victim had to recite the right spell at the correct spot.

There were even routines for getting to fairyland. If you circled a certain Scottish hill nine times between dusk and dawn on Hallowe'en, it was said a door in the hill would open. Enter it and you would be in part of fairyland.

It was believed you could enter fairyland by circling a certain Scottish hill nine times on Hallowe'en.

There are many superstitions surrounding fairies. Anyone unlucky enough to get a visit from a fairy when moving house was in real trouble. Bad luck was inevitable. However, even worse was for an area to lose its fairy population altogether. To guard against this it was necessary to have a good supply of food handy just in case the fairy folk needed it.

And on Hallowe'en, fairies would appear in the homes of people whose ancestors had chased them away many years earlier.

An old music sheet with fairy dancers on the cover.

Witches, spells and fortune-telling

When witches walked

Witches were greatly feared by nearly everyone less than 300 years ago, and by some people in our own century. At Hallowe'en, people believed they were at their wicked worst, and fires blazed across the countryside to frighten them and other evil spirits away.

In Scotland, a more Hallowe'en-gripped country than England, there is a custom of burning a model witch on a bonfire at Hallowe'en. All over the country, though, people used to light bonfires to keep spirits of evil away. Scottish children in Aberdeenshire used to go around collecting fuel for the bonfires and shouting: 'Gie's a peat t'burn the witches' ('Give us peat to burn the witches!'). The fires were supposed to burn the witches as they flew over them on their broomsticks.

Queen Victoria used to enjoy Hallowe'en at Balmoral Castle. There, an effigy of a witch was tried and condemned to be burnt. This 'witch', who had been brought forward to the sound of bagpipes, represented all the bad things that had

Witches are supposed to be at their wicked worst at Hallowe'en.

Four accused witches being 'examined'. In times past, convicted witches were put to death.

happened to the local clan. The evils, supposedly, were burnt with her.

Nobody knows how many hundreds of innocent people must have been burnt over the years. Anyone different – often just old or ugly – might have been suspected of witchcraft, and 31 October must have seen many innocent folk perish.

Accused witches were often strapped into a ducking stool – if they floated in the water, they were guilty; if they sank and drowned, they were innocent.

'Leeting' the witches

A high spot in the anti-witch war took place every year at Hallowe'en at Malkin Tower. This was in the Forest of Pendle in Lancashire. The locals were convinced that witches met there on the big night, so they started a ceremony known as 'leeting' or 'lating' the witches, meaning lighting them.

They believed that if they carried a large lighted candle between 11 p.m. and midnight near the tower, and the flame stayed steady, the witches' power would vanish. But woe betide the idle carrier who let his light go out – or was it blown out by a witch? – as this was supposed to mean bad luck. Naturally, it needed a brave man to carry a candle.

Scotland's great poet, Robert Burns, described in *Tam o'Shanter* what happened to Tam at Hallowe'en. Full of drink, he came upon witches and warlocks (male witches) at a church, with the devil himself playing the bagpipes! The sight of one 'winsome' – pretty – witch among them, made Tam shout for joy. At once, all the lights went out and the witches came after him. He just managed to escape, but his poor horse lost its tail to a witch.

Tam had got half way across a bridge, which made him safe. The horse's tail had been in the wrong half!

The wood from a mountain ash tree, which is called rowan, is believed to protect people from witches. Supposedly, one wave of rowan at even the wickedest witch and you would be safe.

There is an ancient rhyme to remind us of this belief. 'Nag' is a small horse or pony:

> If your whip stock's made of rowan
> Your nag may ride through any town.

Tam o'Shanter and the witches he saw dancing in the church.

Magic fire

Fire! For our ancestors it meant warmth and light. It spelt magic. It could help to ensure that the sun would return after the winter.

All over the world there were – and are – fire festivals and, as we have seen, Hallowe'en is one of them. And Hallowe'en fires mean far more

At Hallowe'en, Lancashire people used to burn straw on the prongs of pitchforks and pray for their dead loved ones.

Stories about the devil and evil doings were told at Hallowe'en.

than ordinary bonfires.

A sacred flame was thought to protect ordinary folk from the powers of darkness. At Hallowe'en in Ireland in ancient times, the druid leaders met at a place called Tlachtga. This was near the holy hill of Tara, the ancient seat of Irish kings. At Hallowe'en, every fire in Ireland was meant to be put out and later lit again from the holy fire of Tlachtga. Then and only then could all be sure of a safe future.

As late as the last century, farmers would walk with their families around their fields holding torches. These they had lit from Hallowe'en bonfires. As long as they did this, so they believed, their crops would grow and their cattle produce calves.

Early in this century in Lancashire, Hallowe'en was called Teanday from 'tan', the Celtic word for light and fire. Straw was burnt on the prongs of pitchforks, as all prayed for their dead loved ones.

Naturally, another reason for bonfires at Hallowe'en was for clearing up refuse and dead vegetation. Farmers knew that ash was good for their soil. Many people believed that light would also help souls in purgatory – the place where the Roman Catholic Church says dead people are forced to stay until their souls are purged of their sins. If they are, it is taught, they can enter paradise. A field near Poulton in Lancashire is called Purgatory, after this belief, and there are other 'purgatory fields' in northern England to this day.

An eighteenth-century picture of people and evil creatures going to the Sabbat – a meeting of the devil and witches.

A torch against evil

Torches and torch-light processions have always been associated with Hallowe'en, especially in Scotland and Wales. The English have tended to concentrate on torches on Guy Fawkes Day.

Farmers used to carry torches through their property at Hallowe'en, and recite spells to protect it through the grim winter months. Children used to hold torches in front of a mirror in a dark room on the big night and say:

> Dingle dingle dowsie, that cat's in the well
> The dog's away to Berwick to buy a new bell.

Alas, nobody now seems to know why they said this!

In Scotland and Wales, 'hallow fire' must have depressed many people. A stone was thrown into the fire and the next day everyone who had thrown one returned to the scene. If someone's stone was still there, all would be well; but a damaged or missing stone meant that the thrower would not live to see the next hallow fire. In some places, the stones were put around the edge of the fire. If any of the stones had moved in the night or been damaged, the 'owner' was thought to be doomed.

Torch-light processions have long been associated with Hallowe'en.

Husband or wife hunting

In olden times, many girls expected to find out what their marriage prospects were at Hallowe'en. So did young men. Those apple pips mentioned earlier was only one of many methods.

A well-loved way of finding out the future, was to bake a cake with a ring, a thimble and a coin in it. The coin meant riches for the finder; the ring meant wedding bells sounding; but the poor thimble finder would never be wed. Of course, he or she could hastily bake another cake!

There is a Norfolk story of six farm workers sitting in a circle and a clean shirt hanging on a pitchfork stuck in the ground. All thought that the loved one of one of them would appear before midnight and take the shirt away. No sweetheart came, so the silly men decided that none of their girlfriends were true to them.

Also, at Hallowe'en, some girls went on to

Many people believed that Hallowe'en was the right time to consult a fortune-teller.

With luck, a girl would see her future husband after sowing hemp seeds.

ploughed land and began sowing hemp seed. 'Hemp seed I sow, who will my husband be, let him come and mow,' they recited. Then they would look over their left shoulder and, with any luck, there would be their future husband.

Some girls also tried the northern England baking method: preparing some dough, without speaking, for a loaf or oatcake called a bannock; then putting the bannock on the baking griddle and going to bed, still in silence. And then, in her dreams, a girl might see her future husband turning the bannock. This 'dumb bannock' method was a feature of Hallowe'en in Cumbria.

In the Scottish Highlands, girls used to find out the size and shape of their future husbands by being blindfolded and then drawing cabbages. That one certainly sounds fun!

More on marriage

Girls tried to discover the trade of their future husbands by dropping molten lead into cold water.

A hundred years ago, teenage girls would put a piece of lead in an iron spoon, then melt the lead over a fire and, finally, pour it into cold water. Why? Because the resulting shape may show what trade their future husbands will have.

There is a Cornish variation of this. Some Cornish folk used to pour molten lead through the hole of the handle of the key to their front door – straight into cold water. Again, a hoped-for husband's trade could be guessed by the shape. Well, sometimes – perhaps!

All sorts of things could be placed under pillows to produce dreams about one's future husband. A sprig of rosemary was popular, and some girls used to take a yew sprig from a graveyard with them to bed. Put under the pillow it, too, might produce a result.

Others believe that Hallowe'en is the right time to consult a fortune-teller, hoping that on this strange night a tall or short, dark or fair, stranger may be spotted – in the cards, on the palm, or even in tea leaves.

Hallowe'en was once called Nut Crack Night in the north of England. A boy and a girl would each put a hazel-nut on a fire and think of each other, saying, 'If he (or she) loves me, pop and fly; if he (or she) hates me, lie and die.' Another nut game predicts the very opposite. If the nuts burn to ashes, a happy marriage is in store for the pair; but should the nuts burst in the flames, things will not be so good.

Games to do with putting hazel-nuts on a fire were popular at Hallowe'en.

A feast of apples

The apple is the most important of all the fruits and plants at Hallowe'en. This is not just because of the games that people play with them – some are described on page 42. Apples were once thought to be a link between men and the gods.

The druids believed in an apple land called Avalon, which was where the immortals lived. Immortal souls had to pass through water to get there. Our link with that fabled past is not so romantic – ducking in water for apples at Hallowe'en! Not that you always have to bob for apples. The Allan apples of Cornwall will give you good luck by just eating them. In St. Ives, Hallowe'en was actually called Allan Day, with 'fairy' apples for sale in a special market. By putting an Allan apple under your pillow, you could dream a wish *and* eat the apple in the morning. Anyone wishing

Apple games have been part of the Hallowe'en fun for hundreds of years.

to live more dangerously can play the game of eating an apple while balancing on a rod of wood, on which there is also a lighted candle.

Yet another use of the fruit was in apple peeling. To play it you first peel your apple, making sure that the peel comes off in one piece. Then you throw your peel over your right shoulder. Look down at the peel and see what letter shape it has made on the ground, and you will know the initial of your future love.

In another apple ceremony, the performer brushes or combs his or her hair in front of a mirror at midnight, while eating an apple. Soon the form of the performer's future husband or wife should show in the mirror. This is just an entertaining game now, but it was not in olden days.

An image of your future partner is supposed to appear in a mirror if you comb your hair at midnight whilst eating an apple.

The night for naughtiness

Mischief Night

Hallowe'en fun and games have quite often gone too far on both sides of the Atlantic. The fact that in Yorkshire, and other northern counties in England, it used to be called Mischief Night, gives us a clue as to why!

Nowdays, Mischief Night has lost a lot of its mischief. In recent times, Mischief Night gradually got shifted to Guy Fawkes' Eve – 4 November. But a century ago, Hallowe'en was the night for naughtiness. And if you could not wait until the next October to be naughty again, there was always May Eve, 30 April.

So twice a year you could smear doornobs with treacle, take doors off their hinges and put fireworks through letter boxes!

The havoc got so bad in some places in past times, with adults joining in as well, that the police had to be called in. Trick-or-treating, so popular in North America, also got out of hand not so long ago and had to be toned down. Trick-or-treat? A trick is played on you if you do not

Taking doors off their hinges was a popular Mischief Night pastime.

Doors were often dumped far away from the scenes of the crimes.

hand a treat over!

Taking doors off their hinges seems to have been a particularly popular Hallowe'en pastime. Sometimes they were thrown into ponds or dumped miles from the scene of the crimes. The day after Mischief Night was a miserable one for many householders, and no doubt still is in some places!

More mischief

In Scotland, high jinks on Mischief Night were allowed to continue for much longer than anywhere else in Britain. Guy Fawkes' Eve and Day are not Scottish festivals, Scotland's Mischief Night being very much a Hallowe'en occasion.

A good game on the night was to climb onto a roof and pile turf into the chimney top. That was a sure way to fill a house with smoke! Smashing

A chimney full of turf was one prank you could expect if you lived in Scotland.

On Mischief Night, Irish and Scottish children used to bombard doors with turnips and cabbages.

bottles was fun, too, just beneath a window. The owners naturally thought that the window had been smashed, but by the time they appeared, the mischief makers were off to do the same again elsewhere.

If you got angry at the tricksters, you were likely to be tormented far more on the next Mischief Night. So, if you live in Scotland and your gate is suddenly removed from its hinges at Hallowe'en, try to remember it is an old British custom. Fortunately, the chances of a smoke-filled house are less because so few people now have proper fires!

Scottish children had extra fun early in our century on Mischief Night, doors being bombarded with turnips and cabbages, and farming implements being removed from farms. Irish children did the same. Many a farmer had to look for his plough, even his cart, on 1 November, All Saints' Day. It must have seemed like 'All Sinners' Day' to them.

Guisers used to put on masks or blackened their faces before roaming parishes demanding money or food.

The guisers

Guisers or guizers, are Hallowe'en characters which have a very long history. 'Guiser' is short for 'disguiser', and disguising yourself is a sensible precaution when you are playing pranks on people. Some say the guisers go back to ancient druid days. Then, the druids blackened their faces for protection with the ashes of a bonfire.

Guising was done by young men and women. They roamed parishes, wearing masks or soot-blackened faces, and they demanded money or food.

In the last century, they improved their image by coming indoors and entertaining people by singing or acting. The guisers were likely to appear at other festivals, and people treated them very well so that they would not come back for a whole year.

Guisers used to sing songs about apples and strong beer, a good tactic to get the householder to give them enough strong drink to 'buy them off' for a year.

Guising lives on in trick-or-treat. The old-time guisers carried the turnip masks and lanterns associated with Hallowe'en. In North America, as we shall see, pumpkins are used instead.

The Hallowe'en masks link our present festival with Samhain and the masked dances that took place in ancient times. Up to a century ago, Scottish guisers looked quite frightening in some areas, the men masked or blackened their faces supposedly to hide them from the dead. They also prevented the living from knowing who was playing pranks on them – like some trick-or-treaters.

A pumpkin is being hollowed out to make a lantern.

Magic lanterns

Hinton St. George in Somerset has a fine-sounding name, and also a fine old Hallowe'en custom. In fact, its great night falls on the last Thursday in October every year, which is only sometimes 31 October. Yet it ranks as one of the most important of all Hallowe'en festivals.

For the village has a festival of 'punkies' and the villagers regard Hallowe'en as Punky Night.

The punkies are Hallowe'en lanterns, made from mangel-wurzels in these parts, not turnips. These are a large type of beet, which cattle eat, and are, of course, hollowed out for the big occasion. Then the candles are put inside the punkies.

These lanterns date back at least to the 1840s. The village women were becoming worried that their men had not returned home from the fields

Pumpkins like this one are made into lanterns at Hallowe'en.

A group of children from Hinton St. George with their punkies.

one Hallowe'en. The men had all the lanterns, so the women decided to make some out of turnips. From that time onwards punkies were made every Hallowe'en, many being marvellous to look at, so cleverly were they designed.

Today, the children of Hinton St. George design and make their own punkies, then parade round the village with them, singing and knocking at doors. They hope to be given a new candle or a coin for their song.

As they go round the village, the children sing:

It's Punkie Night tonight.
Give us a candle, give us a light,
If you don't, you'll get a fright.

It's Punkie Night tonight.
Adam and Eve, they'd never believe
It's Punkie Night tonight.

Hallowe'en in North America

The Puritan past

When people leave home to settle in other countries, they naturally like to take happy reminders of their old life with them. That is what the English, Scottish, Irish and Welsh settlers did when they crossed the Atlantic to North America from the 1600s onwards.

Yet it was not until the last century that Hallowe'en became a popular festival in America. Many of the early settlers had very strict religious beliefs. They did not even approve of celebrating Christmas in an enjoyable way. To these Puritans, as they were called, Hallowe'en was a heathen feast. That ruled out all kind of Hallowe'en

America's early settlers did not celebrate Hallowe'en.

In the last century, the Irish and Scots emigrants brought renewed interest in Hallowe'en to America.

celebrations completely.

In the 1800s, things changed. The Irish and Scots especially, who came in large numbers, did not leave Hallowe'en behind them – and it has been going strong in the United States and Canada ever since. The most famous pastime is trick-or-treating, but there are many others, mostly brought from Britain and Ireland. One is looking into a spring by lamplight to see a reflection of your future husband. Those frightened of the dark should do it in daylight carrying a broken egg in a glass. Pour fresh water into the glass, and soon a man's face is said to appear in the glass. With any luck any children of the coming marriage should appear, too!

Trick-or-treat

Trick-or-treating is the highlight of Hallowe'en for American and Canadian children. It has now become quite popular in Britain, too, where it is like some of the old customs we have seen in this book.

People give trick-or-treaters candy or other treats, so that they will not have practical jokes played on them. They usually pay up! Of course, especially in these sometimes dangerous times, care has to be taken. Traffic can be heavy in the evening, and some cities have areas that are unsafe. Adults usually accompany young children, and light-coloured clothes are often worn so that motorists can see them easily.

Jack-o'-lanterns are a great feature of Hallowe'en in North America. They are hollowed-out pumpkins, which are better than the turnips that British children traditionally use. A spooky face is cut into one side of the pumpkin, and there maybe a candle or other light inside the pumpkin. Masks and costumes are worn for parties and parades, and a marvellous time is had by all.

Jack-o'-lanterns got their name from Jack who, according to an Irish legend, was so mean with his money that he was not allowed into heaven. As he had played pranks on the devil, he was not even allowed into hell! So he is still wandering around, plus lantern, waiting for Judgement Day, when

A dummy and some pumpkin lanterns made especially for the Hallowe'en celebrations.

his luck may change!

Today, many American children collect money for the United Nations Children's Fund – UNICEF – which helps unfortunate children all over the world. It is a fine way to trick-or-treat.

Dressing up is very much a part of trick-or-treating.

Hallowe'en games

The most famous Hallowe'en party games are apple ones. This makes a direct link with the Roman festival of Pomona, mentioned on page 13. So thanks to Pomona a good, and often wet, time can be had by all.

The watery game is bob apple, known as apple dooking in Scotland. Fill a bowl or tub half-full of water and put it on the floor. Then get everyone at the party in turn to try and grip an apple with his or her teeth. There should be a dozen or so apples in the tub. It is not at all easy and there is a sporting chance that every competitor will get more or less soaked! The game goes on, complete with wettings, until every apple in the tub has been eaten. A coin is sometimes stuck in each apple as a prize.

Thanks to the Roman goddess, Pomona, apple games are played at Hallowe'en.

Snap apple is a fun game that can be played by everyone.

Snap apple is fun as well. In this case the object of the exercise is to get your teeth into an apple hanging on a string attached to the ceiling or a beam of wood.

Meanwhile, there is always a chance that apple pies will be part of a Hallowe'en party, also delicious toffee apples. Any Hallowe'en cake should really be decorated with spooky things. The cake is an important part of Hallowe'en, and in olden times Hallowe'en was actually called cake day in parts of northern England. The unfortunate mother had to bake a separate cake for everyone in the family – the sort he or she liked best. Families were usually large in those days!

Farewell to Hallowe'en

As we have seen, Hallowe'en is a strange mixture of opposites – of horror and hoping that your wishes come true. Sometimes the two get mixed up. Not every girl would be prepared to shiver her way into the garden at midnight, pick twelve sage leaves, and wait for a shadowy figure to appear from the other end of the garden. He was meant to be the man she would marry, but at midnight – was it a fiend that approached?

At least, the witches in this rhyme seem quite friendly – or do they?

> Hey-how for Hallowe'en!
> All the witches to be seen,
> Some in black and some in green,
> Hey-how for Hallowe'en!

No wonder in many places lamps were kept burning all night, even in outhouses, just in case.

Today, the festival may just be for fun, but it is easy to understand why our ancestors thought otherwise. With Hallowe'en came the dark months of the year, when it seemed natural for ghosts, demons and witches to be at large, and

Frightening stories of witchcraft and evil spirits were very much a part of Hallowe'en in the past.

creatures like 'Pearlin Jean' – whoever she was!

> She haunts the house,
> She haunts the green,
> And glowers on me
> With her wild-cat e'en.

'E'en' means eyes, and some of our ancestors must have kept their eyes wide open at Hallowe'en – if only to find the quickest way home. From Samhain to trick-or-treat and bobbing for apples gradually, over the years, the fun has replaced the fear.

Today, Hallowe'en is a time for dressing up, taking part in games, and having fun.

Glossary

Celts A group of people who inhabited most of Europe in pre-Roman times.

Druid A priest of the ancient Celts.

Enchanted Under the power of spells.

Fabled Something made famous in a story or legend about mythical characters or events.

Fortune-teller A person who makes predictions about the future by looking into a crystal ball, or reading palms or playing cards.

Heathen A person who is not a Christian, Jew or Muslim.

High jinks Lively enjoyment.

Immortal Something which never dies or is never forgotten.

Mischief Night A night, traditionally at Hallowe'en, on which people play annoying tricks on others.

Pagan Another word for heathen.

Phantom A ghost or ghostlike figure.

Samhain A Celtic festival giving thanks for the harvest at the end of the year.

Superstition A misguided belief in magic and charms.

Trick-or-treat A Hallowe'en custom in America and Canada where children go from house to house demanding a treat or a trick will be forthcoming.

Warlock A male witch.

Will-o'-the-wisp A person or thing that is elusive or misleads.

Further reading

If you would like to find out more about Hallowe'en, you may like to read the following books:

Festivals and Saints Days by Victor J. Green (Blandford Press, 1978)

British Folk Customs by Christian Hole (Hutchinson, 1976)

Highdays and Holidays by Margaret Joy (Faber and Faber, 1981)

Festivals by Jeanne McFarland (Macdonald Educational, 1981)

The Winter Solstace by Shirley Toulson (Jill Norman and Hobhouse, 1981)

The Folklore of the British Isles: a series of books on county folklore from Batsford.

Origins of Festivals and Feasts by Jean Harrowven (Kaye and Ward, 1977)

Index

Acknowledgements

The publisher would like to thank all those who provided pictures on the following pages: Mary Evans Picture Library cover, 4, 5, 8, 12, 13, 15, 16, 19, 22, 26, 27, 38, 39, 42; Sally & Richard Greenhill 11, 23, 35, 36, 40; Outlook Films Ltd. 10; PHOTRI 45; Ronald Sheridan's Photo-Library 44; Malcolm S. Walker 7, 9, 14, 20, 25, 28, 29, 30, 31, 32, 33, 34, 37, 41, 43.